LEWIS

TERESA

ANGEL OF THE SLUMS

CAMPFIRE®

KALYANI NAVYUG MEDIA PVT LTD

Script
Lewis Helfand
Art
Sachin Nagar
Editorial
Suparna Deb, Parama Majumder,
Sourav Dutta, Jason Quinn
Design
Vijay Sharma, Manikandan
Desktop Publishing
Bhavnath Chaudhary
Poster
Sankha Banerjee

www.campfire.co.in

Mission Statement

To entertain and educate young minds by creating unique illustrated books that recount stories of human values, arouse curiosity in the world around us, and inspire with tales of great deeds of unforgettable people.

Published by Kalyani Navyug Media Pvt. Ltd.
101 C, Shiv House, Hari Nagar Ashram, New Delhi 110014, India

ISBN: 978-93-80028-70-5

Printed in India

'When a person dies of hunger,
it has not happened because
God did not take care of him or her.
It has happened because
neither you nor I wanted to give that
person what he or she needed.'

– Mother Teresa

'Come, carry Me
into the holes of the poor.
Come, be My light.'

There are beautiful places in this world. Places filled with light, places where men and women journey to create a brighter future for themselves and their loved ones.
Places that fill your heart with joy and your soul with hope.
But all things have their opposites...
...places where the harsh realities of the world—violence and hatred, poverty and disease—can take control.
So much so that even the gentlest of souls may lose their way in the darkness.
And there were many of these lost souls in Calcutta*, India.
These souls were desperately trying to survive in a place where no one would willingly go...
...almost no one.
*Now called Kolkata.

In those forgotten slums where souls would perish without anyone lifting a finger... there was one woman willing to extend a helping hand. One woman who could not bear to see them suffer.

L-I-leave...
me... alone.
I'm... d-dying.
I'm not leaving you, my child. If you can't walk, I can push you in this cart. But we have to go.
Where?
To hospital. Relax now. We'll be there soon.
This woman is dying. There is nothing I can do to save her. Anyway, we've no spare beds. You'll have to take her to another hospital.
No, I **can't** leave. I **won't** leave. Not until you at least try to help her.
To carry a dying woman from the streets and demand help—what kind of woman was this angel, this savior?
Who was she? Where did she come from?
Why did she want to help? Why could she not turn a blind eye to those in need?

Skopje. 1915.
Mother Teresa was born Agnes Gonxha Bojaxhiu in Macedonia, then part of Albania, on August 26, 1910. From an early age she seemed incapable of denying help to those in need.
Agnes, **help**! We need your help!
Even if it was just helping her big brother, Lazar and older sister, Aga steal jam from the larder.
Warn us if you see Nana coming, Agnes.
Why does this feel so wrong?
If she catches us, we'll be in trouble.
Will you have some jam, Agnes?
No, Lazar. Thank you for asking. The Priest says it's wrong to eat after midnight if you've got Mass in the morning.
Her mother, Dranafile, and her father, Nikola, always taught her the importance of helping others.
Nana Loke*, why do we always invite so many people to come and eat with us?
Because we are blessed, Agnes.
*Mother of My Soul.

'Your father earns more than enough so we should be able to help those in need.'
Hours later.
Papa? Nana says we have more than we need and can share with our neighbors. Is that true?
Yes, it's true Agnes. We have plenty of food, money and nice clothes. So why shouldn't we help others?
Agnes, remember, you should always be happy to share.
Nikola was always donating money and clothing to the poor... sometimes even to complete strangers.
And he was also active politically.
As a member of the town council he always spoke up for minority groups and the underprivileged.

Both he and Dranafile shared their belief in the importance of religion.
In Skopje, Catholics were a small minority and the entire family would pray together every single night.
Whenever Nikola traveled on business, he would return with small gifts.
And this book is for you, Agnes.
It seemed like their family had everything.
Until when Agnes was barely nine, Nikola fell sick on one of his travels...
...and died from internal bleeding soon after returning home.
To add to their misfortune, Nikola's business partner ran off with all their money.

To make ends meet, Dranafile took to embroidering bridal gowns and dresses.
Agnes, I left some bread in the kitchen. I need you to get it and be ready to leave as soon as I finish this dress.
Where are we going, Nana Loke?
You remember the old lady down the road, don't you?
She's not been well. She's all alone now. So we're going to help her with the cooking and cleaning.
I don't know how I would manage without your mother, Agnes. She is such a dear to come here every week.
It wasn't just one neighbor that Dranafile looked after.
She also checked in on a family of six children who had lost their mother.
And she still opened her door to those in need.
She never allowed their own hardships to get in the way of helping others...

...or teaching her children an important lesson.
HA HA HA
My friend told me an even funnier joke at school today. There was this man who tried to kill a fish by drowning it.
HA HA HA
Hey!
What happened to the lights?
Nana Loke, do you know what happened?
I shut off the power. That's what happened.
The three of you are joking around at the dinner table and acting like clowns.
I'm not wasting electricity on foolishness.
If you can't find something worthwhile to do with your time, you can sit here in the dark.

Weeks later...
We can't eat yet, Nana. Lazar isn't here. I'll go get him.
Lazar won't be joining us tonight, Agnes.
Your brother still insists on joking around all the time.
So I sent him to his room without supper.
Now eat your dinner, Agnes.
After dinner...
TAP
TAP
TAP
Lazar? Open up. It's me.
I saved half of my dinner for you.
I know you're being punished but...
...I didn't want you to be hungry.
Thanks, Agnes. I love you so much.

The years passed but daily prayer still played an important part in her life.

One day in 1922...

Nana... there is something that I need to tell all of you.
What is it, Agnes?

I just got a message from God.
He told me to devote my life to Him.
And that is what I want to do.

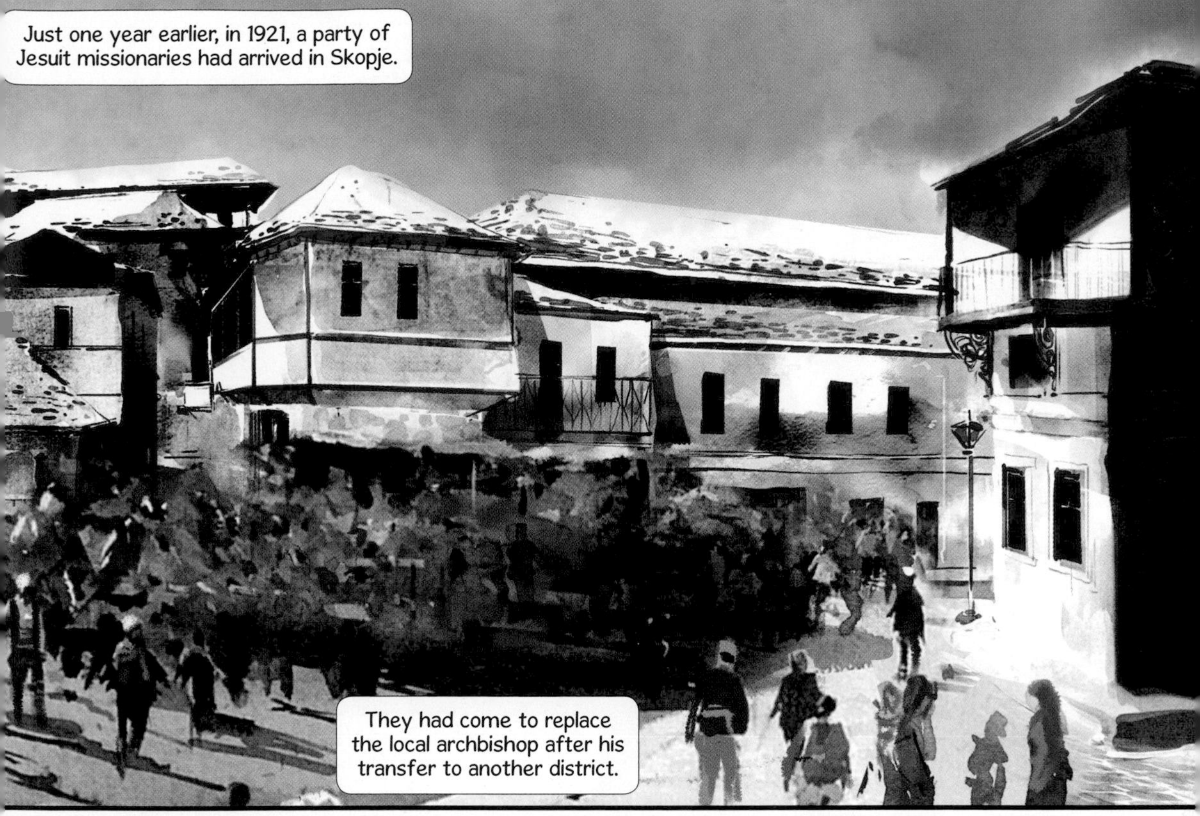

Just one year earlier, in 1921, a party of Jesuit missionaries had arrived in Skopje.

They had come to replace the local archbishop after his transfer to another district.

And they brought with them several stories about their missions to India.
We were in Calcutta for a few months. It used to be the capital of India. It's such a busy, bustling, and joyous place. You'll never see anything like it.
Agnes was captivated by the stories.

I would love to go to India. It sounds exciting.

Few knew of Agnes's desire to visit India. They only saw her as a bright, hard-working student—the top of her class—someone who would always help her classmates with their homework.

But school work didn't inspire Agnes. A different path had captured her attention.

She began spending more time with the missionaries.

They had all spent time in India, in the archdiocese of Calcutta, and they loved sharing their stories.

She started focusing her attention on the missions to India.

No longer content to merely sing in her church choir, she began organizing concerts to raise money for the missionaries.

Then when she turned eighteen...
I'm going to leave Skopje, Nana. I want to become a nun.

No, Agnes, you can't leave. You—you can't leave home to join a convent!
–sob–
Nana? Nana Loke, please open the door.
First my husband died. Then Lazar went away to join the army.
Now I'm going to lose Agnes too.
Oh God, how can I let her go? How can I support her decision?
And yet... if this is what she truly wants... how can I stand in her way?
Dranafile emerged from her room twenty-four hours later.
Agnes? You really believe it is your calling to devote your life to God?
Yes, Nana, I'm sure of it.
Then put your hand in His and walk all the way with Him.

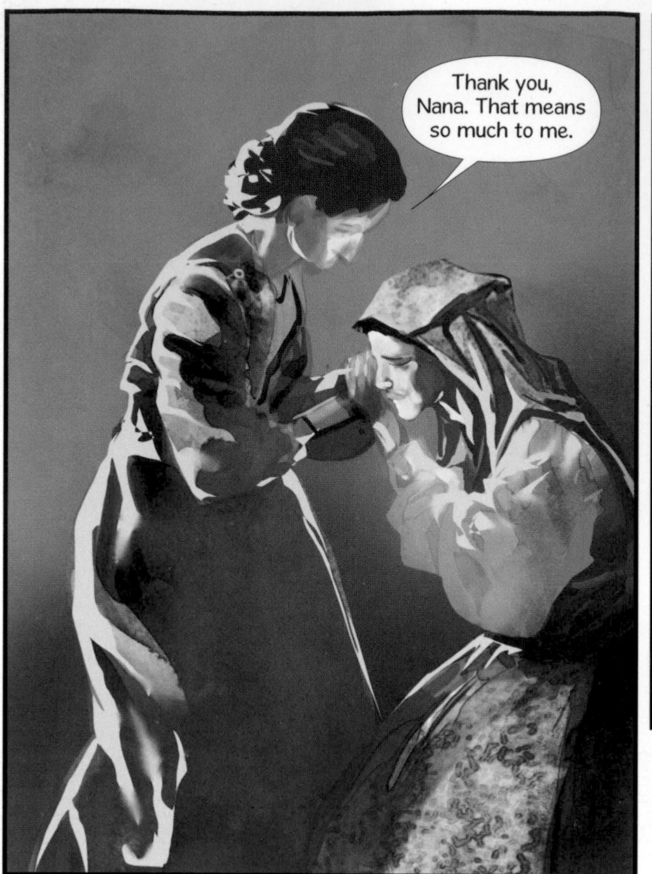
Thank you, Nana. That means so much to me.

Agnes then wrote to her brother asking for his blessing. His reply came quickly.
'My dear Agnes, are you really serious about your decision?'
'How can a lovely girl like you give up everything and move so far away? You might never see any of us again.'

My dear Lazar,
Working for the king of Albania, you shall serve two million people, but I shall serve the king of the whole world.

Agnes enlisted the aid of Father Jambrekovic, one of the local Jesuits who had spoken with Agnes about his missionary work many times.
There's an order of nuns called the Sisters of Loreto.

'They're based in Ireland and also do a lot of missionary work in India.'
'I have spoken about you to Mother Eugene McAvin who runs the French house.'
'She has agreed to interview you. You'll have to go to Paris to meet her. If she feels you are truly devoted...'
'...she will recommend you to Mother Raphael Deasy in Ireland, and you can then travel to the Irish convent for training, and maybe later to India.'

Accompanied by her mother and sister, Agnes left Skopje by train on September 26, 1928.
You must be so excited, Agnes.
I am, Aga. Now I'm finally getting a chance to serve God.
They traveled as far as Zagreb, Croatia, where they met up with another young woman also looking to join the Sisters of Loreto.
Are you Agnes? I'm Betike Kanjc. I'm going to meet Mother McAvin too.
The two girls boarded the train for Paris together.
We love you, Agnes!
We'll miss you!
Do you think Mother McAvin will accept us as nuns, Agnes?
I hope so, Betike.

They had no reason to worry for Mother McAvin was impressed by their devotion.
I had a calling when I was just twelve years old. Six years later, my faith has only increased, and I am still devoted to serving God, Mother McAvin.
Mother McAvin immediately sent them to Loreto Abbey in Rathfarnham, Ireland.
For more than a century, the nuns at that convent had tried to educate young girls in the slums of Ireland and beyond.
And since 1841, the Loreto nuns had been traveling to India to educate the young girls of Calcutta.
Over the next few weeks, Agnes and Betike received a crash course in English. Agnes spoke only Albanian and Serbo-Croat at the time.
In December 1928, they set sail for India.
'I'm leaving my dear house
And my beloved land.
To steamy Bengal go I
To a distant shore.'*
*First verse of a poem written by Agnes on the journey.

One month later, Agnes arrived in Calcutta.
She was thrilled to be in India at last, but was also shocked and unprepared for what she found there.
Those in need lacked far more than even the poorest of the poor back in Skopje.
People were living with no roofs over their heads, no beds to sleep in, and without even the smallest scrap of food to eat.
If our people could see all this, they would stop moaning and thank God for blessing them with such abundance.

As they made their way deeper into Calcutta...
Where will we be staying, Sister?
Well, the two of you will be staying here for a week, after which you both will be going to our Darjeeling center for training.
Agnes and Betike spent a few months in Darjeeling improving their English and even learning the Bengali language. And that was on top of all of their religious training.
I never imagined how much we would have to study. We spend all our day learning our prayers and studying the scriptures and the history of the order.
And now we have to start learning Hindi.
The life of a nun was one of sacrifice. To become a nun one had to go through a trial period of two years, known as a novitiate.
During this time the other nuns had to ensure that Agnes was prepared for the hard life she would have to lead.
So on May 23, 1929...
...Agnes began her novitiate.

Agnes spent the novitiate period learning the mission of the Sisters of Loreto, which focused largely on improving the lives of children through education.
She taught at a small Darjeeling schoolhouse called St. Teresa's.
And she often provided help at a local hospital.
May 24, 1931.
I vow to live a life of obedience and chastity and poverty.
You know that after taking your vows, each nun has to take on a new name.
Betike has chosen the name Sister Mary Magdalen. What name have you chosen, Agnes?
I will be Sister Teresa, Sister Mary Teresa.
Named not after the big Saint Teresa of Ávila, but the little one of Lisieux.
And so Agnes became Sister Teresa. She could now begin her missionary work.

Sister Teresa was sent to a mission hospital in Bengal to assist the nurses.
What is that man carrying?
Oh, my! That poor child... he's just skin and bones!
Sister, this boy is blind and I have nothing to feed him. He was lying in the streets all alone.
If you don't take him in he's as good as dead.
Of course we will take him. This boy has now found a mother.
This was the first time Sister Teresa was directly exposed to extreme poverty and illness.

But the main focus of the Loreto Sisters was not on tending to the sick but on reducing poverty through education...
We are sending you to Calcutta to teach at our convent in Entally.
1931. Loreto Entally, Calcutta.
Sister Teresa was hardly an imposing figure but her actions made an immediate impact on the students.
What is Sister Teresa doing? I've never seen a nun do that before.
Indian society was divided into different castes. And in this caste system, each group held different rights, jobs, and positions.
Sweeping the floors was a task typically performed by those of lower castes.
I don't think Sister Teresa is like the other nuns.
Sister Teresa never saw the world in terms of caste; she just saw those who needed her help and work that needed to be done.
So year after year, she taught history and geography at both Loreto School and St. Mary's—a high school located within the convent walls at Entally.
ASIA
She soon became known as the Bengali Teresa, because she spoke the language so well.

After almost six years of teaching, she took her second and final vows on May 24, 1937.
Today I renew my vows of poverty, chastity, and obedience.
I commit myself to these vows forever.
And I pledge to spend the rest of my life serving God.
And with these final vows, you shall now be known as...
...Mother Teresa.

Now a full nun, she was put in charge of St. Mary's and made principal. She loved every minute of her work, and her students loved her as well.
Good morning, Ma*! How are you today?
*Mother in Bengali.
I'm well, Magdalena. How are you?
I'm good. Subhasini and I can't wait for you to take our history class.
We love your lessons, Ma.
Thank you, Subhasini. I love teaching you all too. And I look forward to seeing you both there this afternoon.
Mother Teresa believed with all her heart that it was her calling to help others.
But it wasn't just Mother Teresa's few hundred students that were in need of a helping hand or a loving heart.
Beyond the towering walls and peaceful gardens of the Loreto compound, an entire city was crying out for help.
And she was beginning to take notice.

Throughout Calcutta, many people lacked even the most basic necessities such as food and shelter.
Whenever she found herself outside the Loreto compound she would come face to face with this poverty.
How can people suffer so much and never break?
And by April of 1942, Mother Teresa's time spent outside Loreto was no longer just an occasional occurrence. It was permanent.
India was under British rule, and in the middle of World War II, the British army needed space that could serve as a military hospital for their wounded soldiers.
Loreto Entally was to be one such spot.
And so the nuns were sent to other convents across the country.
But as for Mother Teresa...

Thank you for staying in Calcutta to teach us, Ma.
Where else would I go? You are my girls. You need to finish your education.
With only a few nuns available, Mother Teresa took on the workload of teaching more classes in little makeshift classrooms a few kilometers away from Entally.
Come along, we have much to learn today.
Ma? Have you noticed there seem to be more and more starving people on the streets lately? What will become of them?
Yes, my child, war only creates more poverty. The ships are being used for the military instead of for delivery of rice. Then the floods wiped out our crops.
We must pray that things get better. There is no telling how many may die of starvation and disease.

After the end of World War II Mother Teresa and her students returned to Entally in 1946.
The situation outside Loreto had grown even worse, with almost two million dead from famine. And if the food shortages weren't bad enough...
...disputes between the Muslim and Hindu communities led to fierce and bloody riots.
Thousands of people were killed.
By this point, the convent was no longer sheltered from the realities of what was happening in Calcutta.
The shops have run out of supplies.
And we are out of food. What can we do?
I can't let my girls starve and suffer. They depend on me.
I will go out and find food.

Mother Teresa had no idea where she would find food and she didn't even know where to look. But she knew she had to try.
Hey! Who are you? Why are you out here?
The rioting streets had become so dangerous that soldiers were constantly on patrol.
The streets are dangerous. You need to get inside immediately. Where do you live?
I live at the Loreto convent.
I need to find some food. We've got nothing.
How many of you are at the convent?
I have a few hundred students. I can't fail them.
My unit is right up there. We've got some rice in our truck. You're welcome to it.
Then we'll take you back to the convent. The streets aren't safe at this time of the night.

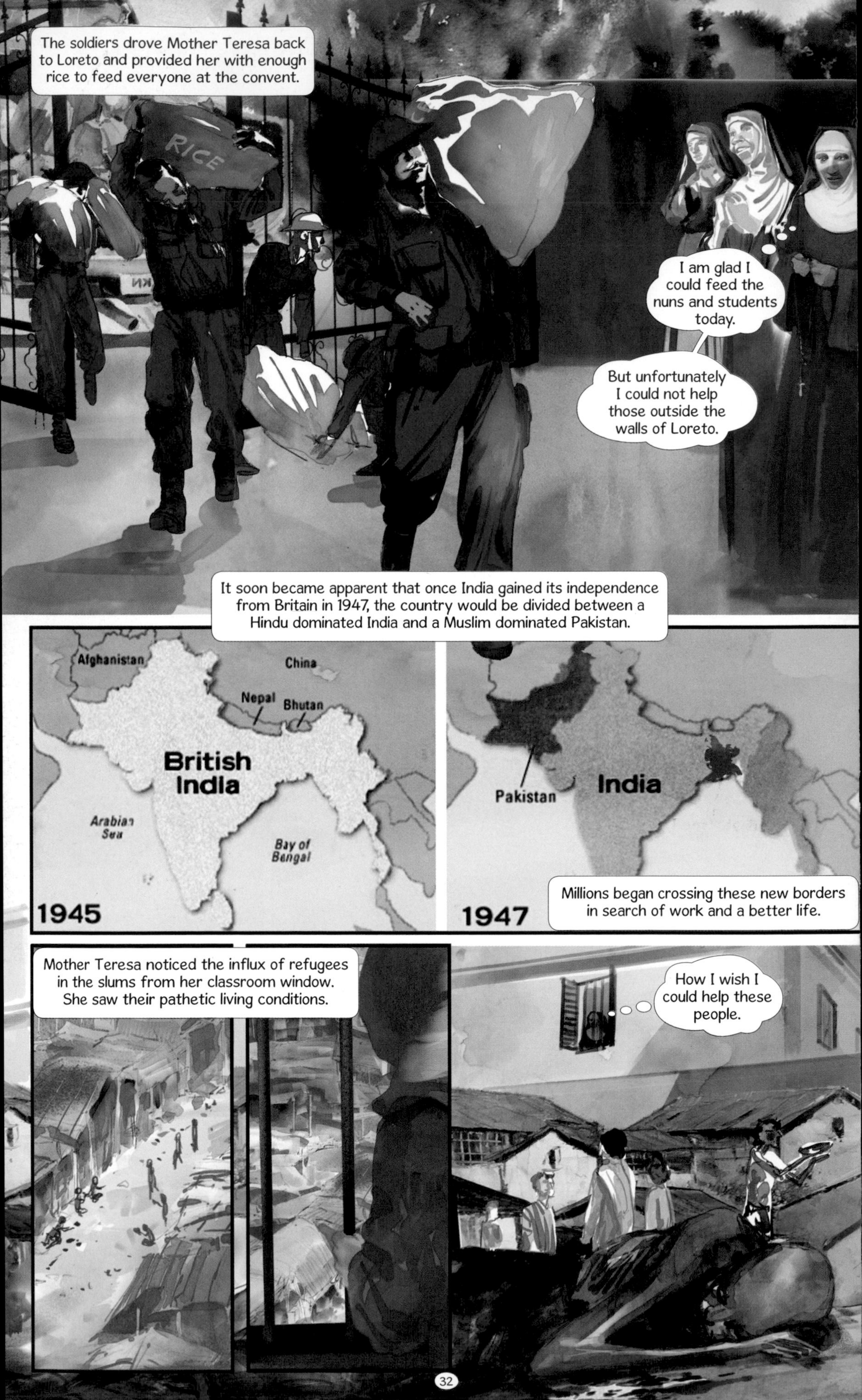
The soldiers drove Mother Teresa back to Loreto and provided her with enough rice to feed everyone at the convent.
RICE
I am glad I could feed the nuns and students today.
But unfortunately I could not help those outside the walls of Loreto.
It soon became apparent that once India gained its independence from Britain in 1947, the country would be divided between a Hindu dominated India and a Muslim dominated Pakistan.
Afghanistan
China
Nepal
Bhutan
British India
Arabian Sea
Bay of Bengal
1945
Pakistan
India
1947
Millions began crossing these new borders in search of work and a better life.
Mother Teresa noticed the influx of refugees in the slums from her classroom window. She saw their pathetic living conditions.
How I wish I could help these people.

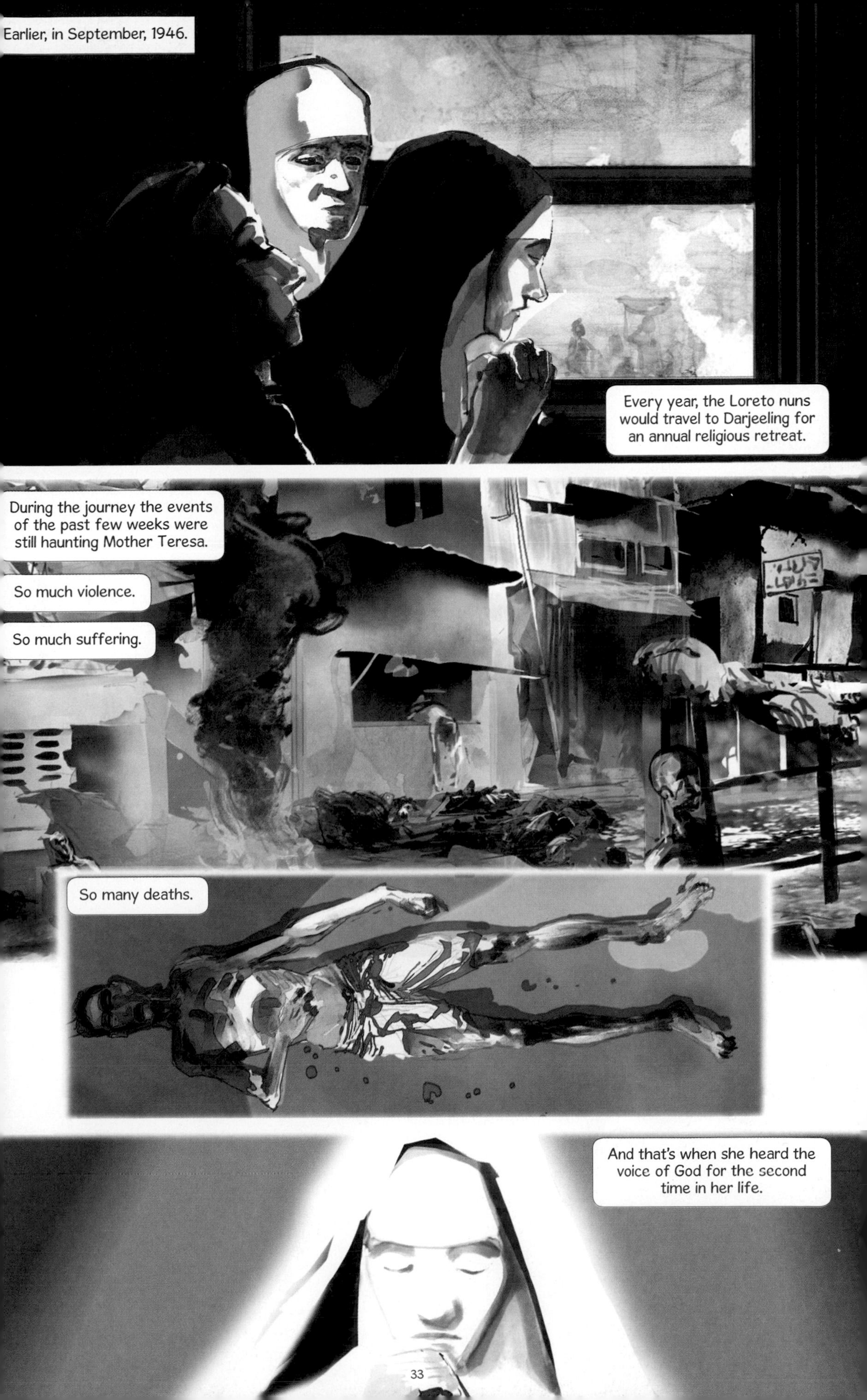

Earlier, in September, 1946.

Every year, the Loreto nuns would travel to Darjeeling for an annual religious retreat.

During the journey the events of the past few weeks were still haunting Mother Teresa.

So much violence.

So much suffering.

So many deaths.

And that's when she heard the voice of God for the second time in her life.

It was a second calling, telling her to leave Loreto, to give up everything, and help the poor while living among them.
She continued pondering over this even after reaching Darjeeling.
Her final vows had included one of obedience. Leaving Loreto would mean breaking that vow.
October 1946. Calcutta.
She chose to approach a local Jesuit, Father Celeste Van Exem, for advice.
Father Van Exem had been Mother Teresa's spiritual advisor since his arrival in Calcutta two years earlier.
You're sure that it was another calling... a call within a call?
Yes, Father. Serving God merely by teaching at Loreto isn't enough. I have to do more.

Nuns aren't allowed to leave the convent. You would have to get special permission from the church.
Give me some time to think about this.

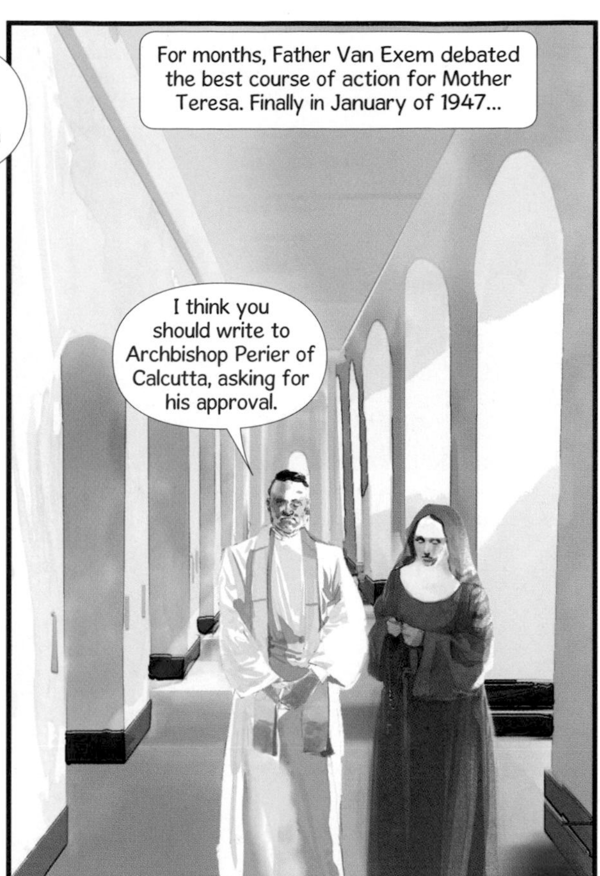

For months, Father Van Exem debated the best course of action for Mother Teresa. Finally in January of 1947...
I think you should write to Archbishop Perier of Calcutta, asking for his approval.

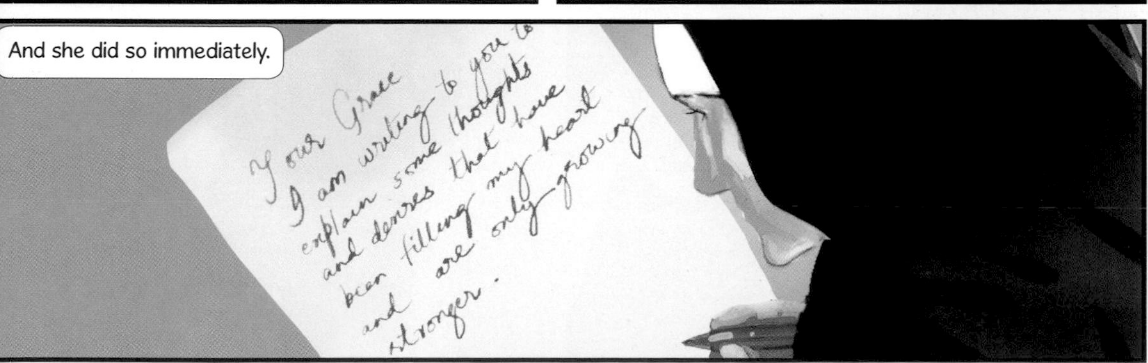

And she did so immediately.
Your Grace
I am writing to you to
explain some thoughts
and desires that have
been filling my heart
and are only growing
stronger.

Mother Teresa had decided not to tell the other nuns at Loreto about her second calling.
Why does Mother Teresa keep meeting with Father Van Exem? Do you think her faith in God is wavering?

Even the senior nuns like the Mother Provincial started doubting Mother Teresa's faith.

Maybe a change of location could make her faith stronger.

You have to go to the convent in Asansol, Mother Teresa.

Asansol was 225 kilometers from Calcutta. It would be the first time since she began teaching at Loreto Entally that she would be separated from her students.

In Asansol, Mother Teresa tended to the convent garden and kitchen, and taught geography. She also continued her correspondence with Archbishop Perier.
How do I convince Archbishop Perier that God wants me to serve the poor?

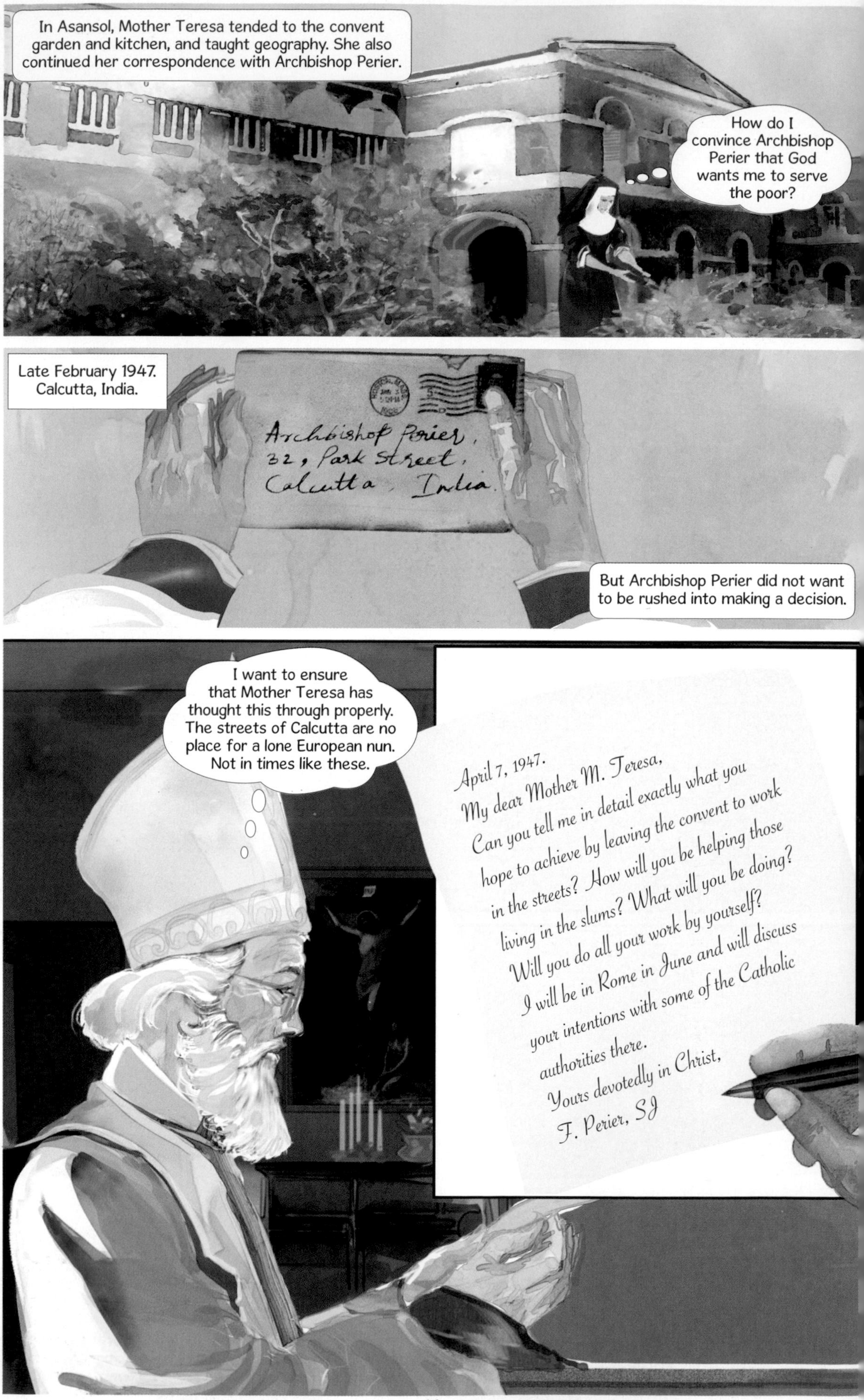

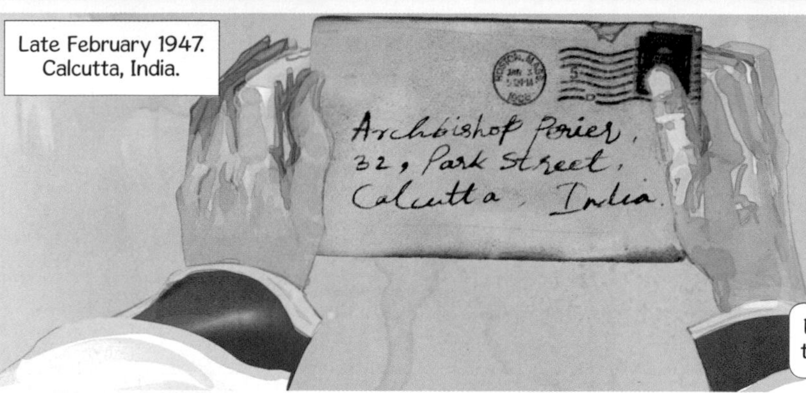

Late February 1947. Calcutta, India.
Archbishop Perier,
32, Park Street,
Calcutta, India.
But Archbishop Perier did not want to be rushed into making a decision.

I want to ensure that Mother Teresa has thought this through properly. The streets of Calcutta are no place for a lone European nun. Not in times like these.

April 7, 1947.
My dear Mother M. Teresa,
Can you tell me in detail exactly what you hope to achieve by leaving the convent to work in the streets? How will you be helping those living in the slums? What will you be doing? Will you do all your work by yourself?
I will be in Rome in June and will discuss your intentions with some of the Catholic authorities there.
Yours devotedly in Christ,
F. Perier, SJ

Mother Teresa wrote back to the Archbishop, explaining how she wanted to help the poor by living in the impoverished slums.
But by mid-June, Father Van Exem advised her that there was still a great deal to consider, and that she should focus all of her attention on her duties as a nun...
...and not on this second calling.
ASIA
Meanwhile at Loreto Entally, the students and the nuns all deeply missed her presence and her bright spirit.
I wish Mother Teresa was still here. Do you think she'll come back?
Mother Teresa proved to be as devoted a nun at the convent in Asansol as she had been in Calcutta.
CALCUTTA
The Superior General of the Loreto Order was convinced there had been some misunderstanding regarding Mother Teresa. They believed she should return to Calcutta.
July 1947. Loreto Entally, Calcutta.
We missed you so much, Ma. Things weren't the same without you.
Please don't leave us again!

Meanwhile, after a year of introspection, Archbishop Perier finally gave his approval on January 6, 1948.

I'm convinced Mother Teresa is serious about her intentions.

But final approval can only come from the Pope himself.

For eight long months, Mother Teresa continued her work at Loreto while waiting for a response from the Pope about her request.

I wonder if my letter got lost in the mail. I must have faith—God's will shall prevail.

August 8, 1948.

Mother Teresa, I have finally received an official answer.

Your request to leave Loreto and help the poor has been...

...approved! You have got an approval for one year and you will report directly to Archbishop Perier.

If for any reason your mission does not work, you will then return to Loreto and resume your duties here.

Father, can I go to the slums now?

Mother Teresa took a week to prepare for her new mission. She thought it was important to live a life of poverty, to not utilize anything the slum dwellers did not use.
Are you looking for some fabric for clothing? I have some beautiful prints to choose from.
I'm looking for something very simple.
She wanted to replace her black habit with the clothing of India, a very basic sari.
This simple fabric will do. I want enough fabric for three saris.
And in keeping with her vow of poverty, she chose the cheapest fabric she could find—plain white cotton with a narrow blue border.
August 16, 1948.
Not wishing to create a scene or suffer any long goodbyes, she left Loreto in the middle of the night with just five rupees in her pocket.
She gave away that money almost immediately to a few needy souls she passed on the street.
And then she made her way to the train station to travel west to Patna.

An order of nuns in Patna had devoted their lives to medical work. Mother Teresa had written to them about her mission, and they offered to give her the medical training she would require.
Mother Teresa? I am Mother Dengel. How much medical training did you say you had?
None, Mother Dengel. I briefly served in a Bengal hospital when I first arrived in India, but I've spent most of my time working as a teacher.
Then we have a lot to show you. Let's begin right away.
If you're going to provide medical care, first you should be able to identify the illness and then know how to treat it.
For example, there are different types of sores. You have to recognize if the sore is from tuberculosis, leprosy, or a common infection.
The medical training was intensive. Mother Teresa soon learned basic medical procedures.
She even sat in on complicated surgical procedures and childbirths. She wanted to be prepared for any type of medical emergency she might come across in Calcutta.

She returned to Calcutta on December 8, 1948. Father Van Exem helped her find a small room at a home for the elderly run by a group of nuns, the Little Sisters of the Poor.
After settling back in Calcutta, Mother Teresa took to the slums.
Moti Jheel lay just outside the Entally compound. It was the very slum Mother Teresa saw from her classroom window during her years at Loreto.
Those brief glimpses had convinced her that this was where she was needed, so she made it her very first stop.
Scenes of poverty and distress were so common that people thought nothing of stepping over the starving or dying as they hurried about their daily business.
Moti Jheel was one of the poorest areas in the entire city. Its residents survived with little food and no medical care or schooling.
For the poorest of the poor there was no relief from suffering.
Those sores on your arms... are they painful?
Y-y-yes... I-I...
Shh. Just rest and let me help you.
Here in this dark, forgotten place... a faint spark of hope glimmered.

The slums of Moti Jheel were not a place for visitors; they were a place where people ended up when they had nowhere else to go.
In such a place, a European nun dressed in a sari truly stood out.
The children were especially curious.
What's she doing?
She looks like a nun. Is she trying to convert people?
Who is she?
I've seen her helping people. And she can speak Bengali.
Mother Teresa saw that the children were not in school. Most of them looked sick, hungry, and neglected. She wanted to help.
The next day.
She decided to look for the children and offer help, since for her, every child was the infant Christ. But a sight stopped her in her tracks.

She wouldn't have to find them. The young children were actually waiting for her at the edge of Moti Jheel.
Still overcome with curiosity, they wanted to see if she would come back again.

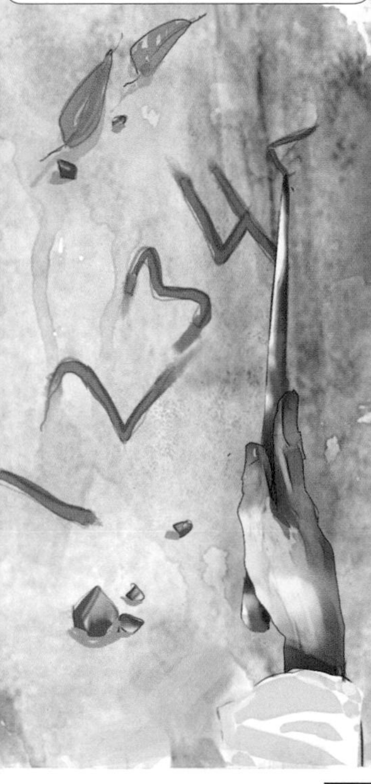
She had no books or any kind of teaching material.
So, with just a wooden stick Mother Teresa began teaching basic arithmetic and writing in her little impromptu open-air school.

A few days later...
Hurry! Hurry! She's back!
Who's back?

Mother Teresa, silly! She's back and wants to teach us more lessons!
The young children were desperate to learn.

By the end of that first week, the lifeless silence of Moti Jheel had been replaced...
...by the lyrical chanting of young voices saying the Bengali alphabet over and over again.
অ আ ই ঈ উ
ক খ গ ঘ ঙ

Days later.
Don't we have class today, Mother? Where are we going?
Of course, we're having class today. But we're going somewhere new.
The Little Sisters of the Poor had donated some money to help Mother Teresa with her work.
She could now buy milk for the children and also rent two empty huts in the slums. One for a school room...
...and one for a shelter for the sick and dying.
But no matter how caring and devoted she was, there was only so much a single person could do.
There were still tens of thousands in the streets and Mother Teresa could not be everywhere at once.
KNOCK
KNOCK

In February 1949, Subhasini Das, one of her former students from Loreto, turned up at the door.
I've come to join you, Ma. I want to help you with your work.
My dear child, you have come from a well-off family and have never known the poverty I am dealing with.
Before I began this work, Father Van Exem wisely asked me to pray and think hard to make sure it was right for me. I ask you to go back and do the same.
And only come back if you are positive this is the life you want.
Weeks later. March 19, 1949.
KNOCK KNOCK
I have prayed, Ma. And I am sure. I want to serve the poor with you.
Thank God.
So Subhasini took the name of Sister Agnes and traded in her expensive saris for the cheapest fabric she could find, just like Mother Teresa.

Magdalena Gomes, another of Mother Teresa's former students, joined them a few weeks later. She took the name of Sister Gertrude.

Then they were joined by yet another former student, and then another, and another.

They spent their nights living together in a small room, and their days in Moti Jheel teaching the young and tending to the sick.

The ones in need of urgent medical care were helped into cabs and rickshaws and taken to hospitals.

No, no, no! Stay away! That woman is sick. She can't sit in my cab.

When they were refused transport...

...they took them to the hospital by whatever means available.

The hospital is full, there's no space left. I can't help her. You'll have to take her back.

She has no home. I found her in the gutter. Can you please try and do something beautiful for God and help her?

I'll see what I can do.

Weeks later...
There is a Hindu family that lives near my house, Mother Teresa.
They have eight children and I know they are struggling and don't have enough to eat.
I don't have the resources to help... I...
Just tell me where they live and I'm sure we can spare some rice for them.
Hours later...
Bless you for bringing us this rice, Mother Teresa.
Is all this rice for us?
Not all of it. I'll just be back.
Moments later.
That rice was for you and your family. Where did you take the rest of it?
I gave half to the Muslim family next door.
They're just as hungry as we are.
The next time, Mother Teresa made sure to send enough food for both families.

In the summer months, Mother Teresa braved the brutal heat, walking the streets endlessly every day.
Her one 'luxury' was to carry a small bottle of water.
Even amidst the monsoons, Mother Teresa's work never stopped. The people outside of the slums began to take notice of her when she would pass.
Not everyone in Calcutta knew her name. They knew of the nun in the white and blue sari that spent her days in the slums. They started calling her the 'Saint of the Slums and Gutters'.
And as word of her mission began to spread, so too did the realization that perhaps the poor and helpless did not deserve to be forgotten and left to their fate.
Small financial donations began coming in from the more well-off citizens of Calcutta. Doctors began volunteering their time and medical services.
How much medicine do you need to purchase today, Mother Teresa?
Purchase? I thought you might want to do something beautiful for God.
I'd love to. Let's call this a donation then. And let me help you carry it out.
Even local pharmacies began to help.

In one year Mother Teresa had achieved far more than expected.

Ten girls, all former students from Loreto, were now working with her.

With the trial year running out, she approached the Archbishop of Calcutta to find out her fate.
Have you heard anything from Rome about whether or not I can continue my work, Archbishop Perier?
No, I have not, Mother Teresa.

The answer came just days later.
Is that from the Vatican? What does it say, Mother Teresa?

Thank God! We have their approval! We can continue our work for another three years.

On October 7, 1950, her small group of nuns became a formal order, just like the Sisters of Loreto.
Our order will be known as the Missionaries of Charity.
Mother, there's a man down that alley in a terrible state. He won't accept any food or drink.
My sister tells me you refuse to eat. Please tell me why.
You can't save me. I don't have the strength to hold that bowl of rice.
Don't worry. I'll hold the bowl for you while you eat.
They worked tirelessly, but poverty and disease continued to spread.

Spring 1952.
The doctor says... he can't save me.
No, hush, don't talk like that. There's a pharmacy down the road. I'll get you some medicines straight away.
I must hurry
But...
Too late. I was too late. Oh, that poor soul.
If I had more resources, could I look after the dying better?
Mother Teresa approached anyone who would listen. She spoke to city officials, even the police commissioner.
POLICE
You can't save everyone, Mother Teresa. Some people are so sick that even the best doctors in the world can't help them.
That may be so. But they don't have to die in the street like animals.
Is there nothing you can do for us? All I need is someone to provide a roof over our heads. My sisters and I will take care of the rest.

In June of 1952, city officials offered Mother Teresa two empty rooms next to a local temple. They were much larger than the shacks in Moti Jheel.
The Kali Temple* is right next door. This room used to be a rest house for pilgrims to spend the night, but it's been vacant for a while. If you think it will meet your needs--
Of course, it will. As I said before, I just need a roof over our heads. My sisters and I will deal with the rest. Thank you.
*A Hindu temple dedicated to the Goddess Kali.
By now, thirty prospective nuns had joined Mother Teresa and many were preparing to take their first vows.
They scrubbed the rooms from top to bottom.
We will name this home Nirmal Hriday*. And now it is up to us to fill the rooms with the helpless.
*Bengali for 'pure heart'.
'We must find those that have no one to care for them.'
'And we must bring them here and provide them with food and shelter and care.'
'We may not be able to cure everyone...'
'...but at least we can ensure they die like angels, loved and wanted.'

October 1952, two months after opening...
The care you are providing here is overwhelming, Mother Teresa.
No one could ever question the pureness of your heart or the work that you are doing.
We're just trying to give them some love and care.
But not everyone was happy with Nirmal Hriday.
They are Christian missionaries. They only want to convert people to Christianity!
So close to the Kali Temple? How dare they?
A group of Hindu men feared their own beliefs were being disrespected by the Christian nuns.
I saw them carry a Hindu priest into their building earlier. Do you think they are trying to convert him?
Yes. And I'm going to put a stop to it right now!

The moment the young man stepped into Nirmal Hriday, he was shocked and overwhelmed by the magnificent sight before him.
This was the most heart-moving example of love and compassion he had ever seen. And it was given to all, regardless of faith or caste.
Of course we convert. We convert you to be a better Hindu, a better Muslim, a better Christian.
Minutes later.
Did you tell them to leave? What happened?
I couldn't, for what I saw...
...I only wish we all had hearts as pure as Mother Teresa and her followers.

We are out of food, Mother Teresa. There is not one grain of rice left.
God will provide what we need.
RICE
The next morning.
Come quickly! Look!
A truck had just arrived from the Calcutta public schools.
Look at all that bread. It can feed us all for days.
Government officials had started taking notice of the work that Mother Teresa was doing.
Word had already spread that the Missionaries of Charity were out of food. So the city of Calcutta shut down their schools for two days.
And they sent all their food to Mother Teresa, so that she could take care of her people.

A few months later...
I found this baby abandoned on the street.
How could anybody abandon her?
'She was lying in the gutter.'
Can anyone tell me whose baby this is? Did something happen to the mother? Do you know--
We don't know, Sister. We just saw a woman abandon a bundle yesterday.
The poor child has no one.
She has us.
There must be so many other unwanted children out there.

They began scouring the streets of Calcutta, searching for abandoned babies.
They found dozens of them, in train stations, alleyways, drains and dustbins.
One day...
Why aren't you two in school? Where are your parents?
We don't have parents. We have nowhere to go.
Well, I'm not leaving you here begging for food in the streets. Come with me.
On September 23, 1955, they opened Shishu Bhavan, a home dedicated to abandoned children.
It's not enough to get these children off the streets. We must find them good homes and prepare them for a life beyond the slums.
Mother Teresa and her nuns even taught the older children skills like typing, embroidery, and carpentry to give them the chance of a better life.

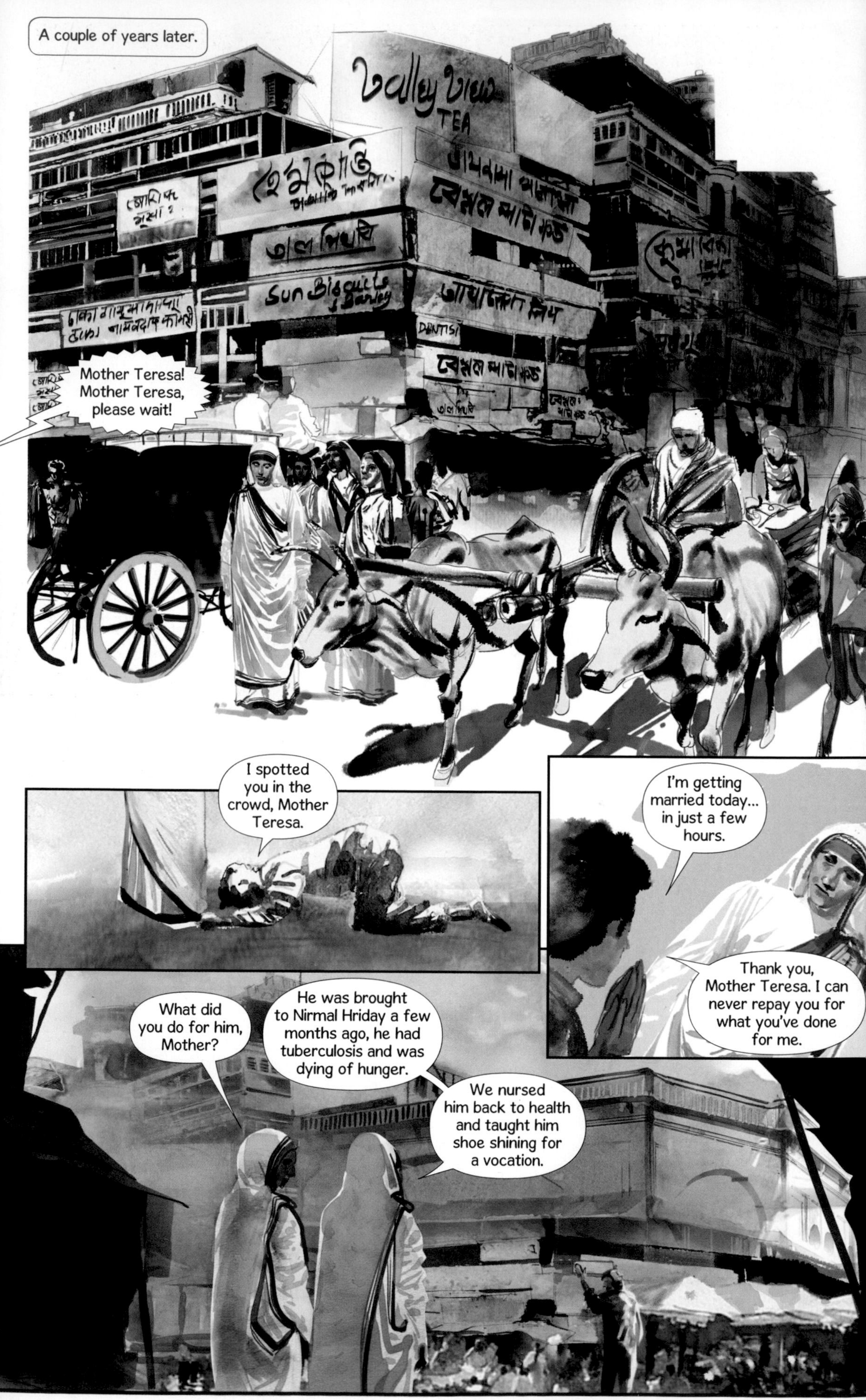

A couple of years later.
Valley View
TEA
Mother Teresa! Mother Teresa, please wait!
I spotted you in the crowd, Mother Teresa.
I'm getting married today... in just a few hours.
Thank you, Mother Teresa. I can never repay you for what you've done for me.
What did you do for him, Mother?
He was brought to Nirmal Hriday a few months ago, he had tuberculosis and was dying of hunger.
We nursed him back to health and taught him shoe shining for a vocation.

We have leprosy.

No one will give us work. Even our families have turned us away. We have nowhere to go. Can you please help us?

Leprosy is a disease that causes nerve damage, and even attacks the skin, creating sores and lumps that are often disfiguring.

And because of their disfigured appearances, people believed that those suffering from leprosy were highly contagious, and shunned them instead of offering help.

There were about thirty thousand people suffering from leprosy in Calcutta alone.
And due to the malnutrition and lack of medical care in the slums, the disease was spreading like an epidemic.
The lepers didn't know then that if detected early, leprosy could be cured. They believed they had no future. No future... until Mother Teresa took up their cause.
With Mother Teresa devoting much of her efforts to help the lepers, others did the same.
Local residents are donating money and medicine and even doctors are offering to help train us to treat leprosy patients.
They even received ambulances to help transport medicine and care to the lepers.
Before the year 1957 was over, Mother Teresa's mission was operating mobile leprosy clinics and treating hundreds of lepers all over Calcutta.
They started distributing food, clothing, and medicines that could help combat the symptoms and even eradicate the disease.

Mother Teresa was offering something much more than medical care.
You will be working with the lepers for the first time, so you should keep a few things in mind.
We should never use gloves. We show the same love and personal touch as we do with our own children.
And remember to smile. Never look upon them with sadness. We are here to give them hope.
Before I contracted leprosy, I had a good job. I-I felt like I was someone... someone important.
My job, belief in myself, it all went away after contracting leprosy.
Now with the care you have shown to us... to me... you've made me feel important again.
That's because you **are** important.
Do you see? The biggest disease today is not leprosy or tuberculosis, but rather the feeling of being unwanted, uncared for and deserted by everybody.

Mother Teresa was really affecting the lives of the poor.
But her activities were limited to Calcutta. There were poor people elsewhere who also needed help and hope.
By 1959...
Who are all those letters from, Mother Teresa?
They are from bishops all over India. They want us to set up houses for the dying and for abandoned children in their cities as well.
And what do you want to do?
I only know one thing... I want to care for those in need.
By the early part of 1960, she set up houses and treatment centers devoted to children, the dying, and lepers in Ranchi and Jhansi.
This particular home will be for the abandoned children, Mr. Prime Minister.
And one in Delhi, where Indian Prime Minister Jawaharlal Nehru paid Mother Teresa a visit for the grand opening of her new facility.
Should I describe my work for you?
No, Mother, I know about it. That is why I have come.

July 1960. Calcutta, India.
Mother Teresa's fame was no longer restricted to India alone.
The requests keep coming in, Mother Teresa.
Requests for what, Archbishop Perier?
Everyone wants you to open up homes for the poor and the dying. And these requests are coming from all over the world.
The work you are doing is worth sharing, Mother. I think you should look into some of these requests.
So Mother Teresa did just that.
On October 25, 1960, she left India for the first time. She traveled all over the world, from the United States and England to Germany and Switzerland.
The place she longed to visit most was Albania, where her family now lived.
Unfortunately she wasn't allowed. Albania was then ruled by a totalitarian communist government that would not allow its citizens to leave or any visitor to enter.

November 1960. Rome, Italy.
While she could not visit her mother and sister, she was overjoyed to be reunited with Lazar, who was now married and living with his wife and daughter in Italy.
I can't tell you how good it is to see you after all these years.
I hear you're opening more mission houses outside of Calcutta.
Yes, by the end of this year, we should have twenty-five houses open all over India.
And what about outside of India?
That's why I'm here.
I plan to open homes outside India, and I need the Pope's approval to do so.

Her meeting with Pope John XXIII was brief. She was awed to be in the presence of the head of the Catholic Church and could request nothing more than a blessing.
She also met other Vatican leaders and spoke about her goals for expansion.
Poverty is everywhere. Even in countries that are far wealthier than India, there is a poverty of the spirit.
They are poor and alone. I believe no one should be alone in this world.
Mother Teresa returned to Calcutta on December 1, 1960.
For the next few years, she continued her work in India, expanding to Agra and Bombay* and Darjeeling.
And she anxiously waited while Vatican officials reviewed every aspect of her order, from the type of medical care they provided to the way the nuns were trained and to the love and care they offered to those who had lost all hope.
*Now called Mumbai.

May 2, 1965. Calcutta, India.
In order to care for the poor, the Archdiocese of Calcutta, some years ago, approved the formation of the Missionaries of Charity.
With the help of God's grace, the Missionaries of Charity has grown much and has sent its sisters into many other dioceses of India to carry out their works.
They had submitted a petition that a 'Decree of Praise' be granted, to allow them to further expand their efforts.
I am pleased to say that our most holy father, Pope Paul VI, gladly received this petition and has awarded the Decree of Praise to the Missionaries of Charity.'
This means that we are now under the direct authority of the Pope.
This is wonderful. It means that no changes can be made to our mission without our consent.
It also meant that they were now free to expand their efforts across the globe.

Worldwide expansion began with South America in Cocorote, Venezuela in 1965.
Mother Teresa? We must first find a location for our Missionaries of Charity house here in Cocorote.
Some locals have been kind enough to offer us a lovely home for our use.
It has a refrigerator and--
Which we graciously have to decline, Sister.
The poor don't have refrigerators and neither should we.
We will find a simple place and live with those in need like we do in India.

And from Venezuela expansion continued rapidly as they spread from continent to continent...
...from Colombo in Asia to Tanzania in Africa and Rome in Europe to Melbourne in Australia and then to New York City in the US, with more than a dozen other cities across the globe in the first decade of expansion.
The one place Mother Teresa was unable to visit was Albania.
Mother Teresa? You said your mother was very ill. Aren't you going to visit her?
I would like nothing more. But the Albanian government won't allow it.
Even if I am allowed into Albania... there is no guarantee I will be allowed to return to India and my mission. I cannot take that chance.
Unfortunately Dranafile passed away in 1972 and Aga died in 1974. Thus Mother Teresa never got her chance of a family reunion.

My dear Mother Teresa
We have never met. I am a priest
in England and I am planning to move to India
to Join the missionaries brothers of charity.
Like you I want to tend to those in the
slums of calcutta.
I think this would be the best use
of my services and I can help the
people most. Can you offer any
advice on how to proceed?

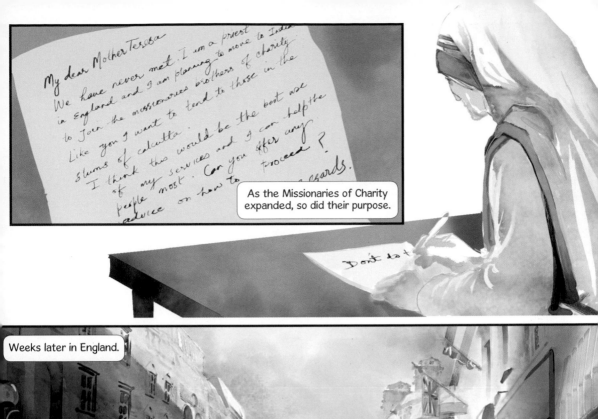

As the Missionaries of Charity expanded, so did their purpose.

Weeks later in England.

'My poor are easy to take care of because they are satisfied with a piece of bread and a cloth to cover their bodies. That's why my work is easier than yours.'

'The poor in your country are poor in spirit. That's why it is harder to get rid of their kind of poverty.'

You look a little down on your luck, my friend. I'd like to help you if you'll let me.

Bless you, Father.

To combat the 'poverty of spirit', the Missionaries of Charity opened houses dedicated to caring for the homeless or alcoholics or shut-ins. Over time, they also focused on helping battered women.
They provided medical care to refugees displaced by wars and famine.
They started doing relief work to help regions ravaged by natural disasters, constructing shelters and rebuilding shattered communities.
And still they never forgot where their work began. Sensing that the lepers she was treating in India needed more care than a mobile clinic could provide, she made leprosy centers.
The first of these centers was built on thirty-five acres of land donated by the Government of India and was named Shanti Nagar, meaning 'town of peace'.
And from this first leprosy center, three hundred kilometers outside of Calcutta, Mother Teresa's order went on to build eighty more.

By 1973, Mother Teresa's order had nineteen homes in thirteen different countries outside of India, and she continued her travels around the world building more and more such houses.
Last year, we opened up homes in Mauritius and Bangladesh and--
Pardon me, Mother Teresa?
We have a seat vacant in first class. Would you like to move there?
That's very sweet of you. But I have no need to travel first class. I'm quite comfortable where I am.
That might be true but...
I... I'm really sorry but we can't do our job.
The other passengers are so excited to see you, they won't stay in their seats.
If you could sit in first class where there aren't so many people, it would make things easier.
After multiple requests, Mother Teresa hesitantly agreed to sit in first class just to help out the airline crew.
In recognition of Mother Teresa's hard work to improve the world, India's national airlines wanted her to have easy access to the entire world and granted her free air travel for life.
And the Indian government even gave her the same privileges on all Indian Railways.

December 11, 1979, Oslo, Norway.
The Norwegian Nobel Committee is pleased to award the Nobel Peace Prize to Mother Teresa for work undertaken in the struggle to overcome poverty and distress.
She is one of those liberated souls who have transcended all barriers presented by race, religion, and nationality. In our present-day troubled world, incessantly plagued by conflict and hatred...
...the work that is carried out by people like Mother Teresa brings new hope for the future of mankind.
I am grateful to receive the Nobel in the name of all those people who feel unwanted, unloved, uncared-for throughout society, people that have become a burden to the society and are shunned by everyone. I hope we can bring love and cheer into their lives.
Mother Teresa also requested the Nobel Committee to cancel the lavish banquet that was to be held in her honor and instead donate that money to feed the poor.
Three months later.
Today, Mother Teresa becomes the first foreign-born recipient of one of India's highest honors, the Bharatratna.
She embodies in herself compassion and love of humanity as few in history have done. Her entire life has been a personification of service and compassion.

Weeks later in Calcutta.
You look like you could use some help.
A bit of food, perhaps? A blanket? What can I give you?
No, I don't want anything. But I have something to give you.
I heard about your work. For all that you do, I wanted to contribute to your cause.
So I decided that whatever I collected today would be donated to your mission.
It's just a few coins but I want to help those less fortunate than I.
Take it. Please. I want you to have it.
There is no limit to the greatness of human kindness.

August 14, 1982.

Demonstrating her compassion again, Mother Teresa visited the city of Beirut in Lebanon to try and aid those affected by a war in the area. The local hospital had been bombed multiple times.

Are there still some patients inside?

Yes, there are thirty-seven handicapped kids inside and we're surrounded by snipers. But even if we could get in and get the children out safely, there is no one to take them.

We have to get them out. **I** will take them. I will take **all** of them!

Do not be afraid, children. Follow me. Everyone stay together. We're going to be just fine.

Mother Teresa herself escorted the starving children from the war-torn hospital and arranged for Red Cross vehicles to transport them to one of the many houses she had established in Beirut.

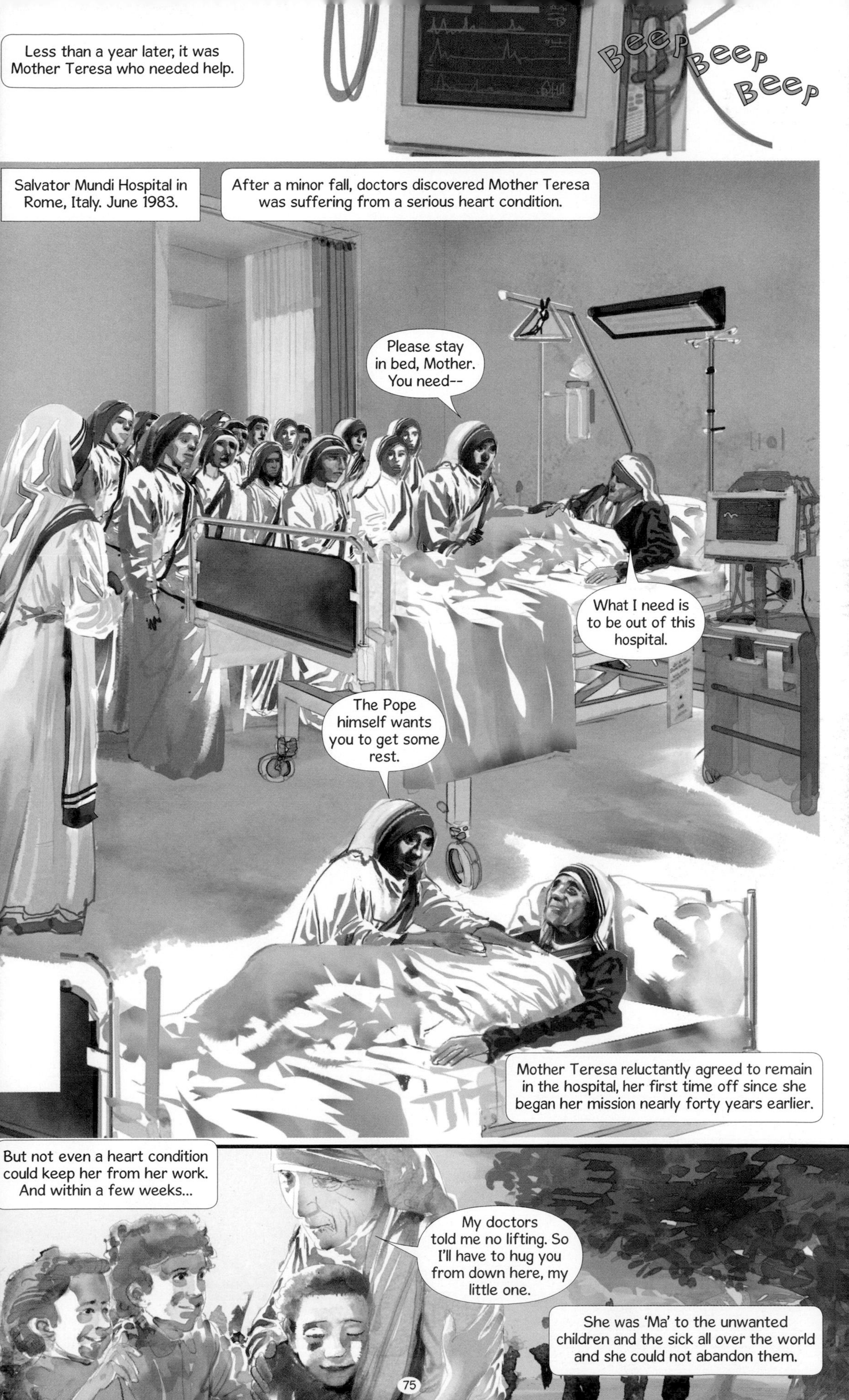
Less than a year later, it was Mother Teresa who needed help.
Beep Beep Beep
Salvator Mundi Hospital in Rome, Italy. June 1983.
After a minor fall, doctors discovered Mother Teresa was suffering from a serious heart condition.
Please stay in bed, Mother. You need--
What I need is to be out of this hospital.
The Pope himself wants you to get some rest.
Mother Teresa reluctantly agreed to remain in the hospital, her first time off since she began her mission nearly forty years earlier.
But not even a heart condition could keep her from her work. And within a few weeks...
My doctors told me no lifting. So I'll have to hug you from down here, my little one.
She was 'Ma' to the unwanted children and the sick all over the world and she could not abandon them.

A grade school in Denmark.

Why aren't any of you having milk today? Did you not bring any money?

We did bring money, but we're saving it to help Mother Teresa.

To help Mother Teresa?
We hear there are children in India that are starving and don't have any milk, and she helps them.

And we thought if we went without milk, we could send our milk money to Mother Teresa.
And she could buy milk for all the children she takes care of.

Month after month and year after year over a hundred thousand Danish schoolchildren went without milk to aid Mother Teresa.

And that same care and concern came pouring into Calcutta from all over the world.
Where did all these boxes come from, Mother Teresa? There are so many. What's inside them?
They came from Canada, Sister. And the boxes are filled with food and vitamins and money.
Who sent them?
Some schoolchildren from Canada. They wanted to help the starving children here in India.
The children have been going on twenty-four hour fast to experience the suffering the children in India endure. And with the money they save they send food to us. They are calling this 'a ton of hunger'.
That's amazing! Why there must really be a ton of food here!
The same care and concern Mother Teresa lived her life by was now being reflected by other caring souls.
Dear Mother Teresa
I'm sending a cheque for a small amount.
I was planning to buy a coat for myself, but
after thinking it over I have decided that
The one I have will last a couple more years.
The cheque is for the amount I would
have spent on the coat.
66921
BRANCH
TWO PENCE

Mother Teresa had received thanks and awards from so many over the years.
But the greatest honor came on February 3, 1986 in Calcutta.
For Pope John Paul II visited her very first home, Nirmal Hriday, to see the work she was doing. He even spoke to each and every patient.
Mother Teresa took me off the streets. I believe I would have died without her.
She is a gift from God.
You have touched so many lives, not just here, but all over the world.
Bless you.

By 1986 she had treated more than four million patients for leprosy alone.
Just a couple of years later the Missionaries of Charity started operating mobile health clinics, six hundred of them. They had by then opened more than 350 houses in seventy-seven different countries.
And they continued to take on new causes... even opening a shelter for AIDS patients.
She traveled wherever she was needed. Whether that was tending to earthquake victims in Armenia...
...or feeding starving children in Ethiopia...
...or comforting radiation victims after an accident at the Chernobyl Nuclear Power Plant.
Even old age and her declining health couldn't slow her down.
She got a pacemaker in 1989. Despite that Mother Teresa remained the head of her order.

Finally in 1991 Mother Teresa succeeded in opening a Mission house in her homeland of Albania, while the world focused on awarding her dedication.
In 1985, she was awarded the US Presidential Medal of Freedom.
In 1993, she was awarded the Pro Ecclesia et Pontifice by the Roman Catholic Church, the most distinguished award offered by the Papacy.
Her prestigious honors often came with not just pins and medals but substantial monetary awards as well, sometimes tens of thousands of dollars. And she donated every cent to the poor.
Pro Ecclesia et Pontifice, 1993
Honorary Order Of Merit, 1983

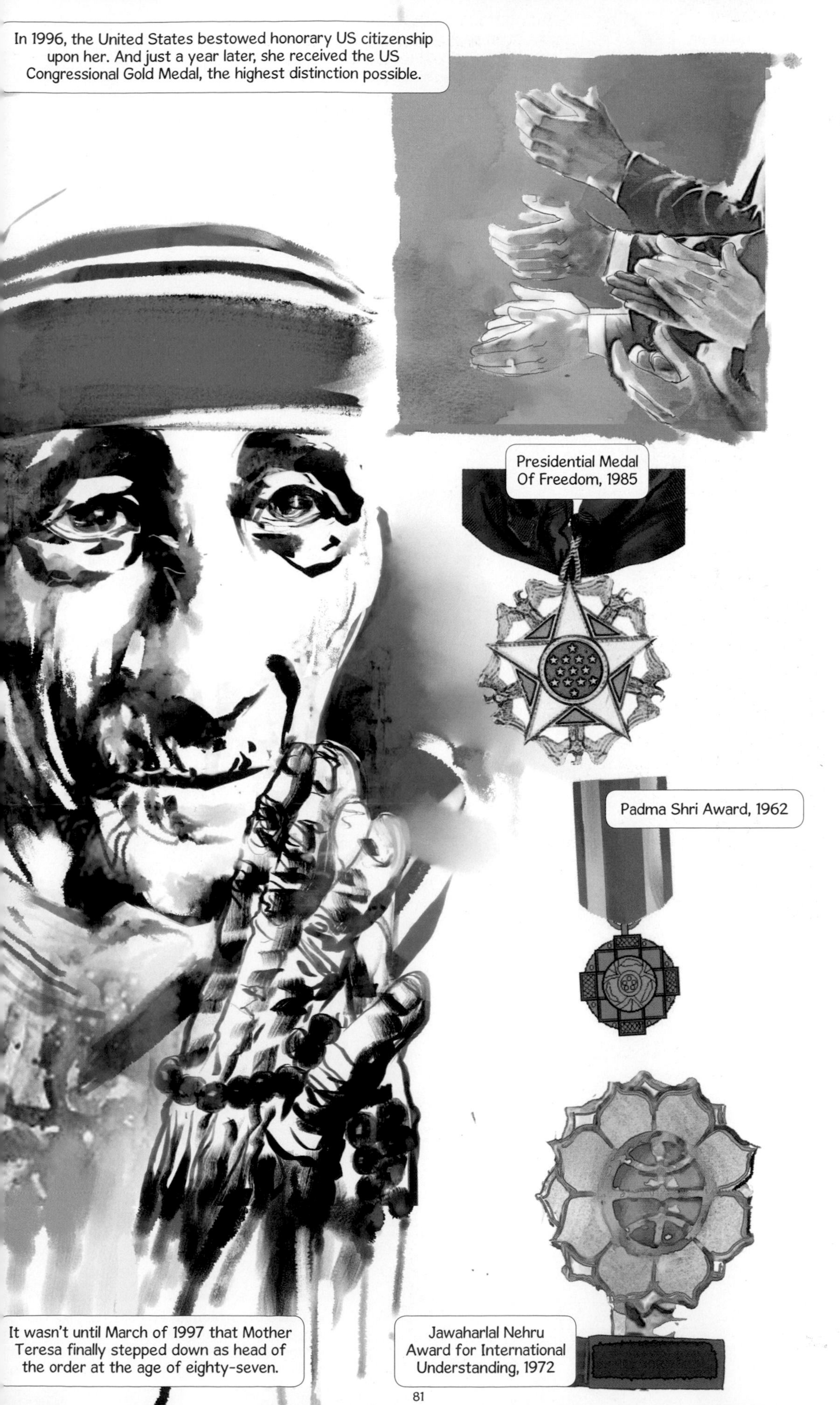
In 1996, the United States bestowed honorary US citizenship upon her. And just a year later, she received the US Congressional Gold Medal, the highest distinction possible.
Presidential Medal Of Freedom, 1985
Padma Shri Award, 1962
It wasn't until March of 1997 that Mother Teresa finally stepped down as head of the order at the age of eighty-seven.
Jawaharlal Nehru Award for International Understanding, 1972

Six months later on
September 5, 1997
her heart gave out.
She was honored with a state funeral.
But death could not end Mother
Teresa's impact on the world.
Six years after Mother Teresa's passing, the
healing of a tumor in the abdomen of a woman in
India was widely believed to be a miracle, caused
by Mother Teresa acting from beyond the grave.

In recognition of that miracle, Mother Teresa was beatified on October 19, 2003. It was the first step to sainthood.
To the people of India and millions all over the world... she already was a saint.
Today there are over 4,500 sisters in 133 countries around the world carrying on Mother Teresa's work as Missionaries of Charity.
When Mother Teresa was born, her family gave her the middle name of Gonxha, meaning rosebud, to reflect how beautiful she was.
But they hadn't imagined at that time how much of an impact her beautiful soul and beautiful spirit would have on the world.
Her selfless devotion to others, her sense of mercy and humility, were beacons of light in this world.
Throughout history, there have been many that have left their mark on the world. Some have changed our lives through their great inventions. Some by leading nations.
And Mother Teresa, she changed the world by sharing her love and compassion and by teaching us to do the same.

Mother Teresa

Small Change

The Government of India issued a 5-rupee coin to commemorate the 100th anniversary of Mother Teresa's birth on August 26, 2010. As you know, it was the sum she had when she left the convent to begin her mission.

Inspiration

So why did Agnes choose the name 'Teresa'? The inspiration came from Saint Thérèse of Lisieux, France. She is known as the saint of missionaries, AIDS sufferers, and orphans. She is also the patron saint of Russia and France.

Thérèse is famous for her compassion and devotion to God, and her emphasis on small daily sacrifices rather than heroic deeds, made her popular among those hoping to lead a spiritual life.

A Nun's Habits

Mother Teresa liked to travel light. Her luggage usually consisted of a small paper package wrapped in string. Even during flights, she never let go of an opportunity to help others; she would ask the stewardess to collect any leftover food, so she could distribute it later to the needy.

Mother Teresa loved writing poetry and playing the mandolin.

The Path to Sainthood

The Roman Catholic Church has over 10,000 saints, but the path to saintliness is long and difficult. Not only must the person have lived an exceptionally holy life, they also need to be responsible for a miracle after death. Once the Pope has approved the beatification of the person, they can now be referred to as 'blessed' but in order to be canonized and become an official saint there needs to be proof of a second posthumous miracle!

Rotten Apples

One day, her mother Dranafile called the young Agnes to the kitchen and showed her a basket full of fresh apples. She then put a rotten apple among them. The next day, she saw that quite a few of the apples were starting to rot. The moral of the story is that it only takes one corrupt individual to spoil all the others, and bad company should always be avoided.

Laughing Matter!

Mother Teresa loved to laugh and was even known to tell a few good jokes. She once told Prince Michael of Greece the following story, 'The other day I dreamed that I was at the gates of Heaven and Saint Peter told me "Go back to Earth, there aren't any slums up here."'

Once somebody asked her if she was married and she replied, 'Yes, and sometimes I find it very difficult to smile at Jesus in the morning because He can be very demanding.'

Mother Teresa over the years. . .

Further Reading on Mother Teresa

Aikman, David. *Great Souls*. London: World Publishing, 1998.

Chawla, Navin. *Mother Teresa: The Centenary Edition*. Delhi: Penguin Books India, 2003.

Gonzalez-Balado, Jose Luis and Janet N. Playfoot, eds. *My Life for The Poor: Mother Teresa of Calcutta*. New York: Harper & Row, 1985.

Kolodiejchuk, M.C., Brian, ed. *Mother Teresa: Come Be My Light*. New York: Doubleday, 2007.

Le Joly, Edward. *Mother Teresa Of Calcutta: A Biography*. San Francisco: Harper & Row, 1983.

Muggeridge, Malcolm. *Something Beautiful for God*. New York: Harper & Row, 1971.

Sebba, Anne. *Mother Teresa*. New York: Doubleday, 1997.

Slavicek, Louise Chipley. *Modern Peacemakers. Mother Teresa: Caring For The World's Poor*. New York: Chelsea House, 2007.

Spink, Kathryn, ed. *Life In The Spirit: Mother Teresa*. New York: Harper & Row, 1983.

Spink, Kathryn. *Mother Teresa*. San Francisco: Harper Collins, 1997.

Vardey, Lucina, comp. *Mother Teresa: A Simple Path*. New York: Ballantine Books, 1995.

Lewis Aaron Helfand

Lewis Aaron Helfand was interested in cartoons, animation, and comics from a young age, and started writing as an amateur from the age of twelve. At twenty-four, he wrote and drew his first independent comic book, *Wasted Minute*. It tells the story of a world without crime where superheroes are forced to work regular jobs. To cover the cost of self-publishing, he began working odd jobs in offices and restaurants, and started exhibiting his book at local comic book conventions. With the first issue received well, he was soon collaborating with other artists, and released four more issues over the next few years.

Lewis also works as a freelance writer and reporter for a number of US print and online publications. He has covered everything from sports and travel to politics and culture for magazines such as *Renaissance*, *American Health and Fitness*, and *Computer Bits*.

Sachin Nagar

After completing his degree in computer applications, Sachin, a resident of New Delhi, India, strengthened his artistic skills by pursuing a diploma in animation, in which he made full use of his technological skills. A highly motivated artist, always seeking to excel, Sachin cites Michelangelo as his one great influence. His artwork for Campfire's Indian mythology titles *Ravana* and *Sundarkaand* has won him great acclaim among critics and comic enthusiasts alike. *Photo Booth*, *The Call of the Wild*, and *Romeo and Juliet* are some of the other titles he has illustrated for Campfire.